Sports Superstars

Shaun Alexander

Football Star

Mary Ann Hoffman

PowerKiDS
press.

New York

Published in 2007 by The Rosen Publishing Group, Inc.
29 East 21st Street, New York, NY 10010

Book Design: Daniel Hosek

Photo Credits: Cover © Harry How/Getty Images; p. 5 © Stephen Dunn/Getty Images; pp. 7, 17, 21 © Jonathan Daniel/Getty Images; p. 9 © Jamie Squire/Getty Images; p. 11 © Andy Lyons/ Getty Images; pp. 13, 19 © Otto Greule Jr./Getty Images; p. 15 © Tom Hauch/Getty Images.

Library of Congress Cataloging-in-Publication Data

Hoffman, Mary Ann, 1947-
  Shaun Alexander : football star / Mary Ann Hoffman.
     p. cm. — (Sports superstars)
  Includes bibliographical references and index.
  ISBN-13: 978-1-4042-3532-9
  ISBN-10: 1-4042-3532-9
 1. Alexander, Shaun. 2. Football players—United States—Biography—Juvenile literature. 3. Running backs (Football)—United States—Biography—Juvenile literature. I. Title. II. Series.
  GV939.A48H64 2007
  796.332092—dc22
  (B)
                                    2006014523

Manufactured in the United States of America

Contents

Shaun Alexander is a running back in the NFL. NFL stands for National Football League.

Shaun plays for the Seattle Seahawks. He set an NFL record of twenty-eight touchdowns in 2005.

7

Shaun was an important player for his college team. He holds the rushing record at his college.

9

In college, Shaun ran many yards and made many touchdowns. He was named Offensive Player of the Year in 1999.

Shaun was a rookie for the Seattle Seahawks in 2000. This means it was his first year in the NFL.

13

Shaun was one of the best rushers on the Seahawks his first year. He rushed sixty-four times for 313 yards!

15

Shaun won the MVP award for the NFL in 2005.

Shaun has played in the Pro Bowl three times. The Pro Bowl is a game played by NFL all-stars every year.

19

The Seahawks played the Pittsburgh Steelers in the 2006 Super Bowl. Shaun proved himself to be a football star!

Glossary

all-star (ALL-STAR) One of the best players in a sport.

award (uh-WARD) A prize or honor given for something you have done.

college (KAH-lihj) A school you go to after high school.

league (LEEG) A group of sports teams.

offensive (uh-FEHN-sihv) Having to do with the players on a team who are trying to score points.

record (REH-kurd) The best or most of something

rush (RUSH) Running with the football.

touchdown (TUCH-down) A score made in football when a player carries or catches the ball over the other team's goal line.

Books and Web Sites

BOOKS:
Gibbons, Gail. *My Football Book*. Singapore: Tien Wah Press, 2000.

Mentink, Jarrett. *Alexander the Great*. Kirkland, WA: Kids in the Clouds Press, 2004.

WEB SITES: Due to the changing nature of Internet links, PowerKids Press has developed an online list of Web sites related to the subject of this book. This site is updated regularly. Please use this link to access the list:
http://www.powerkidslinks.com/spsuper/alexander/

Index